ABOUT THE AUTHOR
CHRIS QUIGLEY

CHRIS QUIGLEY BA (hons), NPQH is a leading trainer of inspectors to the new Ofsted framework. He took up his role as Senior Consultant with Focus after a highly successful headship. He has led two schools through successful OFSTED inspections and was described in October 2001 as "an outstanding leader with exceptional vision. He provides excellent leadership and is the driving force behind the school."

He is qualified as a registered OFSTED inspector and he combines his practical knowledge of leading a school with his awareness of what OFSTED considers to be 'excellent' practice. His ability to convey the sometimes conflicting messages from agencies in a simple, down to earth and practical manner is one of his key strengths that make him an extremely popular speaker and trainer.

Alongside Chris' inspection work he has also led many of Focus' conferences over past terms on a range of topics and is widely becoming a recognised name. His work on curriculum development within the 'Excellence and Enjoyment' agenda is having a major impact on many schools throughout the country and his work extends to the international arena with significant work in Switzerland.

ALSO BY CHRIS QUIGLEY

Accelerate Your Learning In The Literacy Hour

The Behaviour Toolkit

The Assessment for Learning Toolkit

Key Skills for an Excellent and Enjoyable Curriculum

Target Setter - Numeracy

Target Setter - Reading

Target Setter - Writing

Every Child Matters: Writing a SEF that Works

Creativity Toolkits: Key Stage 1

Creativity Toolkits: Lower Key Stage 2

Creativity Toolkits: Upper Key Stage 2

First Published in the UK in 2006 by Focus Education (UK) Ltd

Focus Education (UK) Ltd
Publishing
113-115 High Street
Uppermill
Saddleworth
OL3 6BD

Focus Education (UK) Ltd Reg. No 4507968
ISBN 978-1-904469-43-8

Companies, institutions and other organisations wishing to make bulk purchases of books published by Focus Education should contact their local bookstore or Focus Education direct:

Customer Services
Focus Education, 113-115 High Street, Uppermill, Saddleworth, OL3 6BD
Tel 01457 872427 Fax 01457 878205

Printed in Great Britain by The Studio (Manchester) Ltd, Swinton, Manchester

LEADING YOUR SUBJECT:

INFORMATION & COMMUNICATION TECHNOLOGY

Monitoring Standards and Provisions in **ICT** at Key Stages 1 & 2

Chris Quigley

1. ACHIEVEMENT AND STANDARDS

- What are standards in ICT in your school?
- What does this tell you about achievement?

2. PERSONAL DEVELOPMENT AND WELL-BEING

- How does ICT help children to keep healthy?
- How does ICT help children to stay safe?
- How does ICT help children to enjoy school?
- How does ICT help children to make a positive contribution?
- How does ICT prepare children for future economic well-being?

3. PROVISION

- The quality of teaching
- The curriculum
- Care, guidance and support

4. LEADERSHIP AND MANAGEMENT

- Your track record of making improvements (capacity to improve)
- Action plan

contents

ACHIEVEMENT AND STANDARDS

Schools are now judged on how well children achieve.

We need to know how to measure achievement in ICT. Knowing about standards is the first step. Once we know about standards, we can ask 'are they high enough?'

To work out if children are achieving well, we need to know their *starting points*, their *current level* and the amount of *progress* they make. If we don't know what level our children are at, then we can't ask 'Is that the right level, given their capabilities?'

ACHIEVEMENT

Starting Points

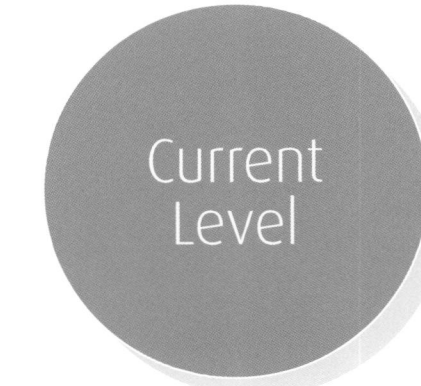
Current Level

Progress

Section 1

ACHIEVEMENT AND STANDARDS

STARTING POINTS

What is the average Foundation Stage profile score at the end of Reception for Knowledge and Understanding of the World?
Make a note below. The table is a *rough guide* to what the profile points mean and the progress we may expect children to make.*

* This is a likely scenario but not necessarily so. Please use this as a rough guide only.

Table 1

POINT	STANDARDS	IMPLICATIONS	OUR AVERAGE POINT SCORE
1			
2	Much lower than expected for a 5 year old.	By the end of KS1 children may be working within level 1.	
3			
4	A bit lower than the expected level for a 5 year old.	By the end of KS1 children may be working within level 2 but are insecure at this level.	
5			Starting Points for children at this school are: *(Highlight as appropriate)*
6	At the expected level for a 5 year old.	By the end of KS1 children should be at least level 2 if they are making satisfactory progress.	• Much lower than the expected level
7	A bit higher than the expected level for a 5 year old.	By the end of KS1 children should be very secure at level 2 and display confidence in the subject.	• A bit lower than the expected level • At the expected level • A bit higher than the expected level • Much higher than the expected level.
8	Much higher than the expected level for a 5 year old.	By the end of KS1 children should be very secure at level 2 and be moving into aspects of level 3, reaching a full level 3 at around the end of Year 3.	
9			

YOU MAY NEED TO DO THIS FOR EACH COHORT IF END OF RECEPTION SCORES DIFFER GREATLY EACH YEAR.

ACHIEVEMENT AND STANDARDS
STANDARDS

Do children cover all aspects of the National Curriculum?

Look at the breadth of study checklist. Which areas are covered well and which areas need attention?

S = Strength   D = Area for Development

KS1 BREADTH OF STUDY	YEAR 1	YEAR 2
Work with a range of information to investigate the different ways it can be presented.		
Explore a variety of ICT tools.		
Talk about the uses of ICT inside and outside the school.		

KS2 BREADTH OF STUDY	YEAR 3	YEAR 4	YEAR 5	YEAR 6
Work with a range of information to investigate the different ways it can be presented.				
Explore a variety of ICT tools.				
Talk about the uses of ICT inside and outside the school.				

ACHIEVEMENT AND STANDARDS

AS A RESULT OF THIS EVALUATION, WHICH **AREAS** DO YOU PROMOTE BEST AND WHAT ARE THE MAIN PRIORITIES FOR DEVELOPMENT?

KEY STAGE 1 STRENGTHS	KEY STAGE 2 STRENGTHS
KEY STAGE 1 AREAS FOR DEVELOPMENT	KEY STAGE 2 AREAS FOR DEVELOPMENT

ACHIEVEMENT AND STANDARDS
DO CHILDREN ACQUIRE THE APPROPRIATE SKILLS?

S = Strength   D = Area for Development

KEY STAGE 1 SKILLS	YEAR 1	YEAR 2
Finding things out • Gathering information from a variety of sources. • Entering and storing information in a variety of forms. • Retrieving information that has been stored.		
Developing ideas & making things happen • Using text, images & sound to develop ideas. • Selecting and adding information that has been retrieved for a particular purpose. • Planning and giving instructions to make things happen.		
Exchanging & sharing Information • Sharing ideas by presenting information in a variety of forms. • Presenting completed work effectively.		
Reviewing, modifying & evaluating work as it progresses • Reviewing work to help develop ideas. • Describing the effect of actions. • Talking about changes to future work.		

DO CHILDREN ACQUIRE THE APPROPRIATE SKILLS?

S = Strength   D = Area for Development

KEY STAGE 2 SKILLS	YEAR 3	YEAR 4	YEAR 5	YEAR 6
Finding things out • Gathering information from a variety of sources. • Entering and storing information in a variety of forms. • Retrieving information that has been stored.				
Developing ideas & making things happen • Using text, images & sound to develop ideas. • Selecting and adding information that has been retrieved for a particular purpose. • Planning and giving instructions to make things happen.				
Exchanging & sharing Information • Sharing ideas by presenting information in a variety of forms. • Presenting completed work effectively.				
Reviewing, modifying & evaluating work as it progresses • Reviewing work to help develop ideas. • Describing the effect of actions. • Talking about changes to future work.				

ACHIEVEMENT AND STANDARDS

AS A RESULT OF THIS EVALUATION, WHICH **SKILLS** DO YOU PROMOTE BEST AND WHAT ARE THE MAIN PRIORITIES FOR DEVELOPMENT?

KEY STAGE 1 STRENGTHS	KEY STAGE 2 STRENGTHS
KEY STAGE 1 AREAS FOR DEVELOPMENT	KEY STAGE 2 AREAS FOR DEVELOPMENT

HOW ARE BASIC SKILLS APPLIED IN ICT?

Children should use the basic skills of communication in its widest sense, they apply their maths skills and they USE their ICT skills to good effect. They should also collaborate, self-evaluate and become creative in their thinking through problem solving activities within the context of ICT.

KEY SKILLS EXPLAINED

COMMUNICATION	Communication involves speaking, listening, reading and writing. Opportunities are provided in English in particular and through pupils' use of language across the curriculum.
APPLICATION OF NUMBER	Application of number includes developing a range of mental calculation strategies and associated mathematical language. Pupils need to develop the ability to use and apply these skills across subject areas and to solve problems in real life situations.
INFORMATION TECHNOLOGY	Information Technology includes the ability to use a range of information sources and ICT tools to find, analyse, interpret, evaluate and present information for a range of purposes across the curriculum.
WORKING WITH OTHERS	Working with others includes the ability to contribute to small-group and whole-class discussions and to work with others to meet a challenge. All subject areas provide opportunities for pupils to share experiences and benefit from what others think, say and do.
IMPROVING OWN LEARNING AND PERFORMANCE	Improving own learning and performance involves pupils reflecting on and critically evaluating their work and what they have learnt, and identifying ways to improve their learning.
PROBLEM SOLVING	Problem solving involves pupils developing the skills and strategies to solve the problems they will face in learning and in life. Pupils need to have opportunities to respond to the challenge of problems and to plan, test, modify and review progress needed to achieve particular outcomes.

ACHIEVEMENT AND STANDARDS
HOW WELL ARE BASIC SKILLS APPLIED IN ICT?

S = Strength   D = Area for Development

	Y1	Y2	Y3	Y4	Y5	Y6
COMMUNICATION						
APPLICATION OF NUMBER						
INFORMATION TECHNOLOGY (How well do children USE their skills?)						
WORKING WITH OTHERS						
IMPROVING OWN LEARNING AND PERFORMANCE						
PROBLEM SOLVING						

WHAT LEVELS DO CHILDREN REACH?

The following tables give an indication of each National Curriculum level.
They also provide planning opportunities for the development of **KEY SKILLS**.

LEVEL 1

FINDING THINGS OUT	DEVELOPING IDEAS & MAKING THINGS HAPPEN	EXCHANGING & SHARING INFORMATION	REVIEWING, MODIFYING & EVALUATING WORK AS IT PROGRESSES

• I can look at lots of different pieces of information.
• I know that information can be shown in lots of different ways.
	• To share my ideas, I:
	  • Use the computer to write
	  • Make pictures on the computer
	  • Sometimes add sounds to my work.
	• I know that lots of things at home and at school work because of instructions.
	• I can get these things to work in different ways by choosing what to tell them to do.
			• I can talk about the way I use ICT

ACHIEVEMENT AND STANDARDS
The following tables give an indication of each National Curriculum level.

LEVEL 2

FINDING THINGS OUT	DEVELOPING IDEAS & MAKING THINGS HAPPEN	EXCHANGING & SHARING INFORMATION	REVIEWING, MODIFYING & EVALUATING WORK AS IT PROGRESSES

• I use ICT to organise information.
 	
• I use ICT to sort information.
 	
• I use ICT to present ideas and things I find out.
 	
• I can save my work.
 	
• I can find my saved work on the computer.
	• I can plan and give instructions to make things happen.
	
	• I can say what happens when I give instructions to a device.
		• I use ICT to share my ideas, or my work in other areas using:
		
		   • Text
		   • Tables
		   • Images
		   • Sound.
		
		• I make improvements to my work (this is called editing).
			• I can talk about how I use ICT:
			
			   • At school
			   • Outside school.

ACHIEVEMENT AND STANDARDS
The following tables give an indication of each National Curriculum level.

LEVEL 3

FINDING THINGS OUT	DEVELOPING IDEAS & MAKING THINGS HAPPEN	EXCHANGING & SHARING INFORMATION	REVIEWING, MODIFYING & EVALUATING WORK AS IT PROGRESSES

• I can save my work.
 	
• I can find my work and other stored information.
 	
• I can use ICT to find the answer to a question.
 	
• I can choose what to do when using software or a website that gives me choices to solve a problem or to find things out.
	• I use ICT to create work.
	
	• I use ICT to develop my ideas.
	
	• I use ICT to organise and present my work.
	
	• I use a sequence of instructions to control devices.
	
	• I use a sequence of instructions to control devices & reach an exact ending.
		• I share my ideas with others by:
		
		  • Opening
		
		  • Reading
		
		  • Replying
		
		  to e-mails.
		
		• I experiment with sound to share my ideas.
			• I describe how I use ICT and its use:
			
			  • Inside school
			
			  • Outside school.

The following tables give an indication of each National Curriculum level.

LEVEL 4

FINDING THINGS OUT	DEVELOPING IDEAS & MAKING THINGS HAPPEN	EXCHANGING & SHARING INFORMATION	REVIEWING, MODIFYING & EVALUATING WORK AS IT PROGRESSES

• I know that I need to be careful when I ask questions when I am:
 	
  • Collecting
 	
  • Finding out information.
 	
• I think about my findings to make sure they are believable.
 	
• I recognise that poor-quality information leads to unreliable answers.
	• I add my own ideas to information I find using ICT.
	
	• I combine different pieces of information from lots of different sources.
	
	• I use ICT to control events in a planned way.
	
	• I use ICT to sense physical data.
	
	• I use ICT models or simulations to:
	
	  • Explore patterns
	
	  • Explore relationships
	
	  • Make predictions about the consequences of my decisions.
		• I use ICT to present information in lots of different ways, including multimedia.
		
		• My work shows that I am aware of the audience.
		
		• My work is of a high quality in its presentation.
		
		• I exchange information and ideas with others in lots of ways, including e-mail.
			• I compare the way I use ICT with other methods *(e.g. how I use ICT to write, find out information, make pictures etc.)*

ACHIEVEMENT AND STANDARDS
The following tables give an indication of each National Curriculum level.

LEVEL 5C

FINDING THINGS OUT	DEVELOPING IDEAS & MAKING THINGS HAPPEN	EXCHANGING & SHARING INFORMATION	REVIEWING, MODIFYING & EVALUATING WORK AS IT PROGRESSES
<ul><li>I select the information I need for the job I am doing.</li><li>I check the accuracy of information.</li><li>I organise information so that I can develop it.</li><li>I use ICT to organise, refine and present information in different forms and styles, including multimedia.</li><li>I use ICT to present my work in a way that is right for the audience and purpose.</li></ul>	<ul><li>I create sequences of instructions to control events.</li><li>I understand that I need to be precise when making and sequencing instructions.</li><li>I understand how ICT devices with sensors can be used to monitor & measure events.</li></ul>	<ul><li>I exchange information and ideas with others in lots of different ways, including e-mail.</li></ul>	<ul><li>I discuss my knowledge and experiences of using ICT.</li><li>I discuss my thoughts on its use both inside and outside school.</li><li>I measure how successfully I use ICT in my work.</li><li>I can use this to make improvements in work that follows.</li></ul>

ACHIEVEMENT AND STANDARDS
STANDARDS AND PROGRESS SUMMARY KS1

What are typical levels of work in ICT by the end of Year 2?

How many children attain levels beyond level 2?

Given the Foundation Stage Profile results at the end of Reception, are children making enough progress? (Refer to table 1.)

Below average progress	Average progress	Above average progress

ACHIEVEMENT AND STANDARDS
STANDARDS AND PROGRESS SUMMARY KS2

What are typical levels of work in ICT by the end of Year 6?

How many children attain levels beyond level 4?

Given the average Year 2 results, are children making enough progress?

Below average progress	Average progress	Above average progress

PERSONAL DEVELOPMENT

HOW DOES ICT PROMOTE CHILDREN'S PERSONAL DEVELOPMENT?

Use the following tables to:

1. Look at the outcomes that are expected for children

2. Make a note of how ICT **in your school** promotes these outcomes.

Note that **not all outcomes** will necessarily be promoted through the teaching of ICT, however the outcomes of ECONOMIC WELL-BEING should be promoted through every subject by:

- Applying basic skills (literacy, numeracy and ICT)

- Promoting creative thinking

- Helping children to become confident risk takers

- Promoting collaboration and teamwork.

Section 2

TO WHAT EXTENT DO CHILDREN ADOPT HEALTHY LIFESTYLES?

OUTSTANDING

- Children have and display an **outstanding UNDERSTANDING** of how to live a **healthy lifestyle.**
- All children take at least **2 hours of PE and sport** each week.
- Many children **involved in physical recreational activities.**
- Whilst at school children **eat healthily.**
- Whilst at school children **drink water** at regular intervals.
- Children (age appropriate) **understand sexual health risks** very well.
- Children **understand dangers of smoking and substance abuse** very well.
- Children are learning very effectively how to **recognise the signs of personal stress and how to manage it.**

GOOD

- Most children have a good understanding of **how to lead a healthy lifestyle.**
- Great majority of children take **2 hours of PE and sport** each week.
- Many children make good use of other opportunities to **extend their physical activity.**
- Whilst at school most **eat healthily.**
- Whilst at school most **drink water** at regular intervals.
- Children (age appropriate) **understand sexual health risks** well.
- Children (age appropriate) **understand dangers of smoking and substance abuse** well.
- Children have a **good understanding** of the symptoms of **personal stress and how to deal with it.**

SATISFACTORY

- Children have a **fair understanding** of how to lead a **healthy lifestyle** shown by:
  - Reasonable participation in PE and sport
  - Sensible eating and drinking habits.
- Children (age appropriate) have a satisfactory understanding of **sexual health risks** but there are **a few gaps.**
- Children (age appropriate) have a satisfactory understanding of **smoking and substance abuse risks** but there are **a few gaps.**
- Children are developing a satisfactory understanding of how to **recognise and deal with mental health problems**, such as **stress.**

INADEQUATE

- **Many children do not have an adequate understanding of what a healthy lifestyle involves, and do not practise one sufficiently whilst at school.**
- A large number of children **do not take 2 hours of PE or sport** each week.
- There is **little organised physical activity** provision beyond PE/sport.
- Eating and drinking in school involves consuming a great deal of **unhealthy food and liquid refreshments.**
- Children have a **weak understanding of sexual health risks** and **substance abuse** risks.
- They are little **attuned to mental health problems**, such as stress, and how to tackle them.

TO WHAT EXTENT DO CHILDREN FEEL SAFE AND ADOPT SAFE PRACTICES?

OUTSTANDING

- Children have and display an outstanding regard for the safety and well-being of others as shown in:
  - Excellent behaviour and attitudes
  - Very low incidence of formal sanctions
  - The sensitive way in which personal dignity is respected.

- Because of the supportive ethos of the school children feel very safe from:
  - Bullying, racism and any other discrimination, and are fully confident that they can confide in and gain strong support from staff should they ever feel threatened.

- Children have a very well developed capability for assessing risks they might face and responding very sensibly to them.

GOOD

- Most children have a good level of concern for the safety and well-being of others as shown in:
  - Restrained behaviour and responsible attitudes
  - Low levels of formal sanctions to secure an orderly community
  - Children show good respect for personal dignity of others.

- Children feel safe from:
  - Bullying, racism and any other forms of discrimination and feel confident in the support available if they feel at risk, knowing they will be listened to sympathetically.

- Children act responsibly when in high risk situations, based on a good understanding of what is likely to be dangerous.

SATISFACTORY

- Children show adequate concern for the safety and well-being of others.

- Despite a few minor exceptions, most children respect the dignity of others and refrain from intimidating or offensive behaviour. Formal sanctions are no more than average.

- Children say they feel safe from bullying and discrimination most of the time and despite occasional incidents that have affected them, or that they know about, they do not come to school in fear.

- Children have reasonable confidence they can get support if troubled by bullying or discrimination, but they feel the school needs to work harder to reduce incidents.

- Most children understand when they are in potentially dangerous situations and respond sensibly.

INADEQUATE

- An unacceptable level of aggressive, insensitive or unrestrained behaviour causes a social environment in which several children report they feel seriously threatened at school and/or many are continuously troubled in more minor ways.

- Many children exhibit little confidence in the school's capacity to help them when in difficulty.

- Children's views are supported by the school's records which show an unacceptable level of bullying and discrimination that needs urgently to be reduced.

- Several children do not have sufficient understanding of potential hazards and they act irresponsibly when in hazardous situations.

HOW MUCH DO CHILDREN ENJOY THEIR EDUCATION?

OUTSTANDING

- Nearly all children have first rate attitudes, and exemplary behaviour.
- Nearly all children have high levels of attendance. They are very punctual to school and to lessons.
- Children co-operate extremely well with staff and others.
- Children readily demonstrate initiative and do not feel intimidated.
- Children take a great deal of pride in their work and involve themselves enthusiastically in their lessons.
- Children are eager to join in other activities outside of lessons.
- Children report very favourably on how well they enjoy school and are excellent ambassadors for it.

GOOD

- Most children enjoy school a great deal as shown in their positive attitudes and restrained behaviour and good consideration of others.
- Attendance is good as is punctuality to school and to lessons.
- Children collaborate readily with others, often take the initiative and feel free from intimidation.
- Children take care in their work and involve themselves well in lessons.
- Children are keen to take part in the school's activities.
- Children say they enjoy coming to school and speak warmly of it.

SATISFACTORY

- Most children enjoy their education reasonably well as shown in their satisfactory attitudes and behaviour, but there may be an absence of obvious enthusiasm or a small number of disaffected learners.
- Attendance and punctuality are satisfactory.
- Children generally feel free from intimidation and comply with rules and requests, though they show only limited enterprise.
- The presentation of work and children's participation in lessons and other activities are adequate.
- Children say they enjoy school.

INADEQUATE

- Many children are disaffected and/or intimidated and do not enjoy school.
- This is shown in unsatisfactory attitudes or behaviour of a significant minority, and the impact it has on others, or by poor levels of attendance and punctuality.
- Children are often reluctant to co-operate with staff, and there is a low level of participation in what the school offers.
- Much work is reluctantly and poorly completed, and children are often disengaged in their lessons.
- Many children speak about the school without affection for it, or are openly hostile to it.

HOW WELL DO CHILDREN MAKE A POSITIVE CONTRIBUTION TO THE COMMUNITY?

OUTSTANDING

- Children make excellent relationships with all in school.

- Children demonstrate a high level of social responsibility by ensuring that their behaviour is not intimidating or offensive.

- Children express their views with much confidence while listening to the opinions of others, and through this make important contributions about how the school runs.

- Children show a great deal of initiative in getting involved in school and community activities, and very readily take on responsibilities for managing aspects of them, so contributing significantly to the range and quality of these activities.

- Children are confident in managing changes in their lives and are developing very well the knowledge and understanding that will enable them to become informed citizens.

GOOD

- Children generally make good relationships with all in school.

- Children's good levels of social responsibility is shown in their consideration and restrained behaviour in their dealings with others.

- Children express their opinions politely but with a determination to be heard, while listening to others, and so contribute effectively to making decisions within the school.

- Many school and community activities flourish due to children's desire to become involved and take responsibility for them.

- Children approach changes in their lives with some confidence, and they are developing well the knowledge and understanding that will enable them to become informed citizens.

SATISFACTORY

- Children make fairly stable and positive relationships with adults and each other.

- With some exceptions, they exercise social responsibility in their dealing with others.

- A fair number of children express their views with confidence, listening tolerably well to others, and thus have some influence on how the school is run.

- Children's willingness to participate in, and take responsibility for school and community activities is satisfactory overall but there might be a minority who do not engage readily.

- Children manage changes in their lives with some independence but need quite a lot of support. They develop a satisfactory knowledge and understanding of the things that will help them to become informed citizens.

INADEQUATE

- Children find it difficult to make stable and positive relationships within school.

- They demonstrate low levels of social responsibility, as shown for example in the extent of the insensitive and intimidating behaviour they display.

- Relatively few have confidence in expressing their views and they are not skilled or tolerant in listening to others.

- Children have little impact on how the school runs.

- Involvement in school and community activities is low.

- Children have little confidence in managing changes in their lives and are not adequately acquiring the knowledge and understanding they will need as citizens.

- Overall, children have an inadequate understanding of their social responsibilities, and a low level of participation in school and community activities.

HOW WELL DO CHILDREN PREPARE FOR THEIR FUTURE ECONOMIC WELL-BEING?

OUTSTANDING

- Children make impressive progress in literacy, numeracy and ICT.

- Through their active involvement in lessons, children develop a strong but not overweening self confidence that empowers them to take initiative and also to work constructively with others.

- Children learn very well how to deal with change and to be creative in their thinking, bold enough to take well-judged risks, and rational in their decision making.

- Children (age appropriate) make very good progress in their financial literacy, and in their understanding of the business and economic environment.

GOOD

- Most children make good progress in literacy, numeracy and ICT.

- They develop a good level of self-confidence and strong team working skills, which is demonstrated by the initiative and involvement they demonstrate in classroom and other activities.

- Children learn how to cope with and plan for change, as seen in the open-endedness of their thinking, their measurement of risk and their ability to justify their decisions.

- Children (age appropriate) make good progress in their financial literacy and the business and economic environment.

SATISFACTORY

- Children make steady progress in literacy, numeracy and ICT.

- Many acquire the self confidence to take the lead occasionally and work adequately with others most of the time, as shown by the level of interaction in lessons.

- Children develop a satisfactory understanding of how to deal with change, to think of alternative solutions and to calculate risks involved with certain lines of action.

- Children give generally adequate reasons for the decisions they make.

- Children (age appropriate) make satisfactory progress in their financial literacy and how business and the economy work.

INADEQUATE

- A significant number of children do not make adequate progress in literacy, numeracy and ICT.

- Children do not develop adequate self-confidence and the capacity to work with others, as shown by their passivity or lack of co-operation in lessons.

- Children do not become adequately enterprising, and understand poorly how to deal with change, to look for alternatives, to take measured risks, and to make reasoned decisions.

- Children (age appropriate) make inadequate progress in their financial literacy.

PERSONAL DEVELOPMENT
HOW IS CHILDREN'S PERSONAL DEVELOPMENT PROMOTED THROUGH ICT?

AREA	HOW IS IT PROMOTED	GRADE
BEING HEALTHY		
STAYING SAFE		
ENJOYING		
POSITIVE CONTRIBUTION		
ECONOMIC WELL-BEING		

1 = outstanding 2 = good 3 = satisfactory 4 = inadequate

HOW IS CHILDREN'S PERSONAL DEVELOPMENT PROMOTED THROUGH ICT?

Example (NOT an exemplar)

AREA	HOW IS IT PROMOTED	GRADE
BEING HEALTHY	• All children drink plenty of water in ICT lessons. • Children are aware of their own learning styles and teachers give children outstanding opportunities to demonstrate their understanding in their own preferred ways. Children consider not just what they learn but HOW they learn, which helps them to be independent and they say this makes them feel less stressed.	1
STAYING SAFE	• Children understand the importance of sitting on a proper computer chair and having a break when looking at a screen.	2
ENJOYING	• Children say they enjoy ICT – especially the use of ICT in other subjects. • Children take pride in their work and speak of their own progress in ICT skills with enthusiasm.	2
POSITIVE CONTRIBUTION	• Children gain a good understanding of how some of their presentations are intended for the differing needs of audiences. This helps them to become **informed citizens.**	2
ECONOMIC WELL-BEING	• Children apply literacy, numeracy in all ICT work well and this helps them to make rapid progress in these areas. • Children are given good opportunities to solve problems in finding out activities and in their presentations.	2

1 = outstanding 2 = good 3 = satisfactory 4 = inadequate

THE QUALITY OF PROVISION

PROVISION SHOULD BE JUDGED IN TERMS OF THE OUTCOMES IT LEADS TO.

The 3 areas of provision are:

1. Teaching and learning

2. The curriculum and other activities

3. Care, guidance and support.

> Provision is good if it leads to good ACADEMIC and PERSONAL development for ALL children.
> If outcomes are not good, then we must ask whether provision is good.

Section 3

WHAT IS TEACHING HELPING CHILDREN TO DO IN THEIR PERSONAL DEVELOPMENT?

If you are saying teaching is: Then children should....	BEING HEALTHY	STAYING SAFE	ENJOY	MAKE A POSITIVE CONTRIBUTION	ECONOMIC WELL-BEING
OUTSTANDING TEACHING	Drink water at regular intervals. Learn very effectively to recognise signs of personal stress and strategies to deal with it.	Excellent behaviour. Excellent attitude to work.	First rate attitudes. Exemplary behaviour. Very good co-operation. Take initiative. Take interest and pride in work. Eager to join in, punctual to lessons.	Excellent relationships. High level of social responsibility (behaviour). Express views with much confidence, listening very well to others.	Impressive progress in basic skills. Active involvement in lessons. Take initiative. Creative thinking. Rational in decision making.
GOOD TEACHING	Most drink water at regular intervals. Understand symptoms of personal stress and deal with it.	Restrained behaviour. Reasonable attitudes.	Positive attitudes. Restrained behaviour. Take care over work. Involved in lessons, punctual.	Good relationships. Restrained behaviour. Express opinions politely, listening to others.	Good progress in basic skills. Good level of self confidence. Strong teamwork. Open ended thinking, justifying decisions.
SATISFACTORY TEACHING	Sensible drinking habits.	Adequate concern for safety and well-being of others. Refrain from offensive behaviour.	Satisfactory attitudes, behaviour and punctuality. May be an absence of obvious enthusiasm. Adequate presentation of work.	Stable and positive relationships. Generally adequate behaviour. Take part in lessons but some who don't readily engage. A fair number express views confidently.	Steady progress in basic skills. Work adequately with others in lessons. Adequate ability to think of alternative ways. Offer adequate reasons.
INADEQUATE TEACHING	No water available or taken at regular intervals.	Unacceptable level of aggressive behaviour/minor troubles.	Many children disaffected or intimidated. Unsatisfactory attitudes of significant minority. Poor punctuality lack of co-operation, disengaged. Poorly completed work.	Few positive relationships. Low levels of responsibility: poor behaviour. Unskilled in expressing views, don't listen to others.	Significant number do not make adequate progress in basics. Low self confidence. Passive or uncooperative. Unenterprising.

WHAT IS TEACHING HELPING CHILDREN TO DO IN THEIR ACADEMIC DEVELOPMENT DURING KS1?

If you are saying teaching is: Then children should....	ICT SKILLS	BASIC SKILLS
OUTSTANDING TEACHING	Children are good in all respects and exceptional in some. Exceptional means that they go far beyond a good level.	Children are good in all respects and exceptional in some. Exceptional means that they go far beyond a good level.
GOOD TEACHING	Children make good progress. They use ICT to organise and classify information and to present their findings. They enter, save and retrieve their work. Children plan and give instructions to make things happen and they describe the effects. Children use ICT to help them generate, amend and record their work. They share their ideas in different forms, including text, tables, images and sound. Children talk about their experiences of ICT both inside and outside school.	Children make good progress. Children **communicate** using the full range of writing styles that they have learned in their English lessons. They listen to others well and carefully present their thoughts. Children use their **counting, calculation and data skills** to record and interpret their own and others' observations.
SATISFACTORY TEACHING	ICT skills are not inadequate, in other words, they are all done to some extent to a level that is reasonable. Some skills may be good, but not all of them. As a result, children make steady progress. (A reasonable level means children can do it but confidence is lacking.)	Basic skills are used to some extent but tend to rely on verbal communication rather than written or pictorial. Some data is used but it is patchy and calculation and counting skills are not thoroughly developed.
INADEQUATE TEACHING	If any of the aspects described in the good section are not taught, or if they are taught in a way that leads to a lack of understanding, then children will not make enough progress and this is inadequate.	If any of the aspects described in the good section are not taught, or if they are taught in a way that leads to a lack of understanding, then children will not make enough progress and this is inadequate.

WHAT IS TEACHING HELPING CHILDREN TO DO IN THEIR ACADEMIC DEVELOPMENT DURING KS2?

If you are saying teaching is: Then children should....	ICT SKILLS	BASIC SKILLS
OUTSTANDING TEACHING	Children are good in all respects and exceptional in some. Exceptional means that they go far beyond a good level.	Children are good in all respects and exceptional in some. Exceptional means that they go far beyond a good level.
GOOD TEACHING	Children make good progress. They understand the need for care in framing questions when collecting, finding and interrogating information. Children interpret their findings, question plausibility and recognise that poor quality information leads to unreliable results. Children add to, amend and combine different forms of information from a variety of sources. Children use ICT systems to control events in a predetermined manner and to sense physical data. Children use ICT models and simulations to explore patterns and relationships, and make predictions about the consequences of their decisions. Children use ICT to present information in different forms and show they are aware of the intended audience and the need for quality in their presentations(including multimedia). Children exchange information and ideas with others in a variety of ways, including using e-mail. Children compare their use of ICT with other methods and with its use outside school.	Children make good progress. Children **communicate** using the full range of writing styles that they have learned in their English lessons. They listen to others well and carefully present their thoughts. Children use their **counting, calculation and data skills** to record and interpret their own and others' observations.
SATISFACTORY TEACHING	Skills are not inadequate, in other words, they are all done to some extent to a level that is reasonable. Some skills may be good, but not all of them. As a result, children make steady progress. (A reasonable level means children can do it but confidence is lacking.)	Basic skills are used to some extent but tend to rely on verbal communication rather than written or pictorial. Some data is used but it is patchy and calculation and counting skills are not thoroughly developed.
INADEQUATE TEACHING	If any of the aspects described in the good section are not taught, or if they are taught in a way that leads to a lack of understanding, then children will not make enough progress and this is inadequate.	If any of the aspects described in the good section are not taught, or if they are taught in a way that leads to a lack of understanding, then children will not make enough progress and this is inadequate.

THE QUALITY OF PROVISION
SUMMARY OF THE QUALITY OF TEACHING

KEY STAGE 1	KEY STAGE 2
The quality of teaching is........................ because:	The quality of teaching is........................ because:
STRENGTHS	STRENGTHS
AREAS FOR DEVELOPMENT	AREAS FOR DEVELOPMENT

THE QUALITY OF PROVISION
THE QUALITY OF THE CURRICULUM

Like teaching, the quality of the curriculum is judged on outcomes.

A good curriculum leads to good academic and personal development.

THE QUALITY OF PROVISION

HOW DOES THE ICT CURRICULUM HELP CHILDREN IN THEIR PERSONAL DEVELOPMENT?

If you are saying your curriculum is... then children will....	BEING HEALTHY	STAYING SAFE	ENJOY	MAKE A POSITIVE CONTRIBUTION	ECONOMIC WELL-BEING
OUTSTANDING	Very effective recognition of personal stress in their ICT work and how to manage it.	Outstanding regard for safety. Very well developed capacity to judge risks during visits.	Children report very favourably how well they enjoy ICT.	Confident in managing changes in their lives. Developing very well the knowledge and understanding that will enable them to become informed citizens. Great deal of initiative getting involved in school and community activities.	Very good self confidence and team working skills.
GOOD	Good understanding of personal stress in their ICT work and how to deal with it.	Good regard for safety. Act responsibly in high risk situations during visits.	Children report they like ICT.	Some confidence in managing changes in their lives. Developing well the knowledge and understanding that will enable them to become informed citizens. Desire to get involved in school and community activities.	Good self confidence and team working skills.
SATISFACTORY	Satisfactory understanding of personal stress in their ICT work and management strategies.	Adequate concern for safety. Understand potentially dangerous situations during visits.	Children say they enjoy ICT.	Satisfactory willingness to become involved in activities but some not readily engaged. Some independence in managing changes in their lives but need quite a lot of support. Satisfactory knowledge and understanding that will enable them to become informed citizens.	Adequate self confidence and team working skills.
INADEQUATE	Little attuned to stress in their ICT work and how to tackle it.	Insufficient understanding of potential hazards during visits, acting irresponsibly.	Many children speak about ICT without affection for it.	Children have little impact on how the school runs with low involvement in activities. Show little confidence in managing changes in their lives. Not acquiring the knowledge and understanding they will need as citizens.	Poor self confidence and team working skills.

HOW DOES THE ICT CURRICULUM HELP CHILDREN IN THEIR ACADEMIC DEVELOPMENT DURING KS1?

If you are saying your curriculum is... then children will....	ICT SKILLS
OUTSTANDING	Children make rapid progress in their ICT work. All aspects described below are done well and some are done exceptionally well.
GOOD	Children make **good progress** in their ICT work. They learn to: • Work with a range of information to investigate the different ways it can be presented • Explore a variety of ICT tools • Talk about the uses of ICT inside and outside the school.
SATISFACTORY	Children make steady progress and have a reasonable understanding of the above but lack confidence in some areas. They may understand some aspects to a good level but not all. Nothing is inadequate.
INADEQUATE	If any of the above outcomes are missing, then children will not be making adequate progress in their ICT work.

HOW DOES THE ICT CURRICULUM HELP CHILDREN IN THEIR ACADEMIC DEVELOPMENT DURING KS2?

If you are saying your curriculum is... then children will....	ICT SKILLS
OUTSTANDING	Children make rapid progress in their ICT work. All aspects described below are done well and some are done exceptionally well.
GOOD	Children make **good progress** in their ICT work. They learn to: • Work with a range of information to investigate the different ways it can be presented • Explore a variety of ICT tools • Talk about the uses of ICT inside and outside the school.
SATISFACTORY	Children make steady progress and have a reasonable understanding of the above but lack confidence in some areas. They may understand some aspects to a good level but not all. Nothing is inadequate.
INADEQUATE	If any of the above outcomes are missing, then children will not be making adequate progress in their ICT work.

THE QUALITY OF PROVISION
SUMMARY OF THE QUALITY OF THE CURRICULUM

KEY STAGE 1	KEY STAGE 2
The quality of the curriculum is......................... because:	The quality of the curriculum is......................... because:
STRENGTHS	STRENGTHS
AREAS FOR DEVELOPMENT	AREAS FOR DEVELOPMENT

THE QUALITY OF PROVISION

CARE, GUIDANCE AND SUPPORT

The main things we are concerned with in this section are:

- The feedback children get about their work

- The advice they get on how to improve

- The progress children make.

As with teaching and the curriculum, if guidance is good then outcomes must be good.

THE QUALITY OF PROVISION
THE QUALITY OF GUIDANCE

GRADE	DESCRIPTION
OUTSTANDING	Children make much better progress than would be expected. All aspects of feedback are good and in some areas, it is exemplary. Children know what they need to work on in the future.
GOOD	Written feedback is focused on objectives and any success criteria. It shows children what they have done well and what they need to do to improve this piece of work further. Children get a chance to respond to this feedback and this helps them to improve their work. Verbal feedback highlights how well children are getting on with the lesson objective and gives advice as to how to improve. As a result, children make good progress.
SATISFACTORY	Written and verbal feedback gives general comments about the work and there may be some examples of good practice, but this is not widespread. Children get some opportunity to respond to feedback but not always and it leads to only satisfactory progress.
INADEQUATE	Children do not know what they do well and get very little guidance as to how they can improve their work. This contributes to slow or inadequate progress.

THE QUALITY OF PROVISION
SUMMARY OF THE QUALITY OF GUIDANCE

KEY STAGE 1	KEY STAGE 2
The quality of care, guidance and support is........................ because:	The quality of care, guidance and support is........................ because:
STRENGTHS	STRENGTHS
AREAS FOR DEVELOPMENT	AREAS FOR DEVELOPMENT

LEADERSHIP AND MANAGEMENT

Effective leaders improve standards of children's:

- Academic Development

- Personal Development.

It is important that you can demonstrate your track record in improving standards.
The following questions should guide you in your work:

- Do I know what standards and children's well-being in ICT are?

- How do I find this out?

- What does this tell me about achievement?

- What am I doing to improve standards?

> This book has guided you through this process so far. The following pages give a suggested format for improving outcomes for children.

Section 4

MY TRACK RECORD OF IMPROVING STANDARDS AND ACHIEVEMENT

WHAT DID MY MONITORING TELL ME?	WHAT DID I DO ABOUT IT?	THE IMPACT WAS

LEADERSHIP AND MANAGEMENT
ACTION PLAN FOR ACADEMIC DEVELOPMENT

OUTCOMES TO IMPROVE	ACTIONS TO IMPROVE PROVISION			
ACADEMIC DEVELOPMENT	TEACHING & LEARNING	CURRICULUM	CARE & GUIDANCE	LEADERSHIP & MANAGEMENT
	Actions	Actions	Actions	Actions
	Cost & source of funding	Cost & source of funding	Cost & source of funding	Cost & source of funding
	By when	By when	By when	By when
	Who will lead	Who will lead	Who will lead	Who will lead
	Monitoring milestones	Monitoring milestones	Monitoring milestones	Monitoring milestones

LEADERSHIP AND MANAGEMENT
ACTION PLAN FOR PERSONAL DEVELOPMENT

OUTCOMES TO IMPROVE	ACTIONS TO IMPROVE PROVISION			
PERSONAL DEVELOPMENT	TEACHING & LEARNING	CURRICULUM	CARE & GUIDANCE	LEADERSHIP & MANAGEMENT
	Actions	Actions	Actions	Actions
	Cost & source of funding	Cost & source of funding	Cost & source of funding	Cost & source of funding
	By when	By when	By when	By when
	Who will lead	Who will lead	Who will lead	Who will lead
	Monitoring milestones	Monitoring milestones	Monitoring milestones	Monitoring milestones

INFORMATION FOR THE SCHOOL'S SEF

STANDARDS IN ICT ARE	
THE SOURCES OF EVIDENCE FOR THIS ARE	
THIS MEANS THAT ACHIEVEMENT FOR CHILDREN IS	
BECAUSE	
THIS IS WHAT WE ARE DOING TO IMPROVE STANDARDS AND ACHIEVEMENT	